I DO! I DO!
THE MARRIAGE VOW
WORKBOOK

Create inspiring marriage vows that will . . .
express your deepest feelings for one another,
increase your trust and connection,
and provide a strong foundation for your relationship,
now and in the years to come.

SHONNIE LAVENDER
& BRUCE MULKEY

I Do! I Do! The Marriage Vow Workbook

Address all inquiries to:

Shonnie Lavender & Bruce Mulkey
16 Spears Avenue, #19
Asheville, North Carolina 28801
info@marriagevowworkbook.com
www.marriagevowworkbook.com

Editor: Susan Snowden, Snowden Editorial Services

Cover art and design: David Lynch, Lynch Graphics

Author photographs: Steve Mann, Black Box Photography

ISBN-10: 1-84728-038-2

ISBN-13: 978-1-84728-038-1

Published by Lulu Press

July 2006

To Tom and Sharon Parish, who during their eighteen-year marriage,
modeled profound love and steadfast commitment,
and who during Sharon's recent passing,
modeled undeniable grace and courageous letting go.

Sharon Parish passed from her mortal form at the age of forty-nine on May 31, 2006.
To learn why we loved this remarkable woman so much, visit the weblog created by
her husband and our cherished friend, Tom Parish: http://sharonparish.typepad.com.

*I was on a train on a rainy day. The train was slowing down to pull into a station. For
some reason, I became intent on watching the raindrops on the window. Two separate
drops, pushed by the wind, merged into one for a moment and then divided again—
each carrying with it a part of the other. Simply by that momentary touching, neither
was what it had been before. And as each one went on to touch other raindrops, it
shared not only itself, but what it had gleaned from the other.*

~Peggy Tabor Millin

Table of Contents

TIPS ON STAYING TOGETHER

*Make a list of things your partner likes and
do one at least once a week.*

*Put a picture of both of you at your wedding
where you can look at it often.*

If you see a booger on your partner's nose, pick it off.

Learn to say "I'm sorry" and "Will you forgive me?"

Breathe, breathe, breathe.

Try to wear out your sense of humor.

Don't say anything rude about your partner's mother.

Don't go to sleep with your backs to each other.

Keep in mind: you are each other's mirror.

Have fun; life is short.

~Tom & Sharon Parish presented this wisdom
to the authors as a wedding gift in July 1999.

Praise for *I Do! I Do! The Marriage Vow Workbook*

This creative workbook will be valuable to any couple planning their marriage or re-commitment. Furthermore, the post-ceremony guidance will help them transform their wedding into their marriage. I highly recommend it.

> ~Harville Hendrix, Ph.D., author of *Getting the Love You Want: A Guide for Couples* and cocreator of Imago Relationship Therapy

During the magical ceremonies we call weddings, we recite vows with passion and proclaim our love to the world. Yet we may not always LIVE these words with the same passion for the rest of our married lives.

When Bruce and Shonnie chose to become married, they made conscious choices about their wedding weekend, their marriage vows, and how they would live their lives based on their souls' commitments to one another. In doing so, they created a loving, fulfilling, and enduring relationship in which they are LIVING their vows—encouraging each other to live boldly, authentically, compassionately, and courageously. In I Do! I Do! The Marriage Vow Workbook, *they offer their lived wisdom to couples who wish to follow a similar path.*

My work is to help people see the sacredness in all relationships—especially in business—and this is what the workbook that Shonnie and Bruce have created does so brilliantly for couples. Not only will The Marriage Vow Workbook *empower couples to write vows that express the love they share, it will awaken them to a more mindful, connected, and authentic way of being together . . . now and for all their days.*

> ~Lance Secretan, Ph.D., award-winning author (*ONE: The Art and Practice of Conscious Leadership*), speaker, coach, and advisor to leaders

As a psychologist who works with couples, I intend to use I Do! I Do! The Marriage Vow Workbook *with my clients who are about to get married and also with those in couples therapy. Often folks in a relationship are unhappy because they have gotten off course or drifted from their initial vision for living together joyfully. They begin looking for a way out or for a way back to the magic that once held them together in a sacred commitment. Whether couples want to create a commitment or make a re-commitment, it takes a thoughtful, step-by-step process that looks exactly like the one so beautifully designed and guided by Shonnie and Bruce in* The Marriage Vow Workbook.

> ~John E. Hoover, Ph.D., psychologist

"YES, YES!" is our response to I Do! I Do! The Marriage Vow Workbook *by Mulkey and Lavender. Anticipating that this workbook was for persons who intended to get married some time in the future, we started our review of it through the eyes of a married couple of some years. We really did not expect to find help for our already committed relationship. But that changed in a matter of minutes! By the time we finished the exercise at the end of Chapter 3, we realized our assumptions about the workbook were shortsighted. As we continued to evaluate the chapters and exercises, we found ourselves saying, "We should try this exercise or that ritual. We wrote our own marriage vows years ago, but how long has it been since we've looked at them? Do we even know where they are?" When we completed our review of the workbook, we embraced its insights for our relationship.*

What we discovered in I Do! I Do! *is a thought-provoking and uncompromising message for couples who want to create a conscious, committed relationship. Whether marriage is in the future, has already happened, or may never happen, this workbook is a means to move relationships more toward the good for which we all yearn.*

~Helen Bruch Pearson, Candler School of Theology, Emory University (Ret.)
and Luther E. Smith, Jr., Ph.D., Professor of Church and Community,
Candler School of Theology, Emory University

Shonnie and Bruce have truly created this workbook out of their own powerful and inspiring relationship. I Do! I Do! The Marriage Vow Workbook *is a must-do for thoughtful couples who want to prepare well for a marriage that will last a lifetime.*

~Ken and Elizabeth Loyd Kinnett, founders of Back to Bliss™ Relationship Workshops

This workbook should be required reading for any couple contemplating marriage, for the probing and insightful questions are best explored with a partner far in advance of the wedding day. The information gleaned could prove priceless.

~Paul Howey, author of *Freckles: The Mystery of the Little White Dog in the Desert*,
winner of the ASPCA Henry Bergh Children's Book Award

Thank you so much for creating this workbook. Using it to write our marriage vows has been a wonderful experience for us. Not only has it helped us to produce vows that really fit, it has encouraged us to consciously address some issues in our relationship as well as develop a compelling vision for our future. We're both deeply grateful for your work.

~Allison Jordan and Gil Holmes

The Marriage Vow Workbook is a spiritual tool for creating joyful and loving marriages which, in turn, promote peace in the world. As Confucius said:

> *If there is righteousness in the heart, there will be beauty in the character.*
> *If there is beauty in the character, there will be harmony in the home.*
> *If there is harmony in the home, there will be order in the nation.*
> *If there is order in the nation, there will be peace in the world.*

We give this useful and transformative workbook five stars and recommend it highly to all who embark on this sacred journey.

~Mary Page Sims and The Rt. Rev. Bennett J. Sims, Bishop of the Episcopal Diocese of Atlanta, 1971-1983

As a minister who officiates at seventy to eighty weddings each year, and as one who truly believes in committed love, I know how helpful this book will be. First-time marriages or second- and third-time-arounders will find this guide wonderfully helpful in designing just the right words for celebrating their love. A big Yes! to Mulkey and Lavender for enhancing one of the most powerful and important experiences a couple can have together.

~Rev. Howard Hanger, Founder and Minister of Ritual & Celebration, Jubilee! Community Church, Asheville, NC

Couples who engage this book fully will come out of the process knowing their partners, themselves, and their relationship more deeply. The questions posed here, the context offered, and the stories shared will do nothing less than enrich their lives. Bruce and Shonnie offer hard-won wisdom, encouragement, and guidance that we haven't found anywhere else. This is a generous book.

~Deanna LaMotte and David LaMotte, singer-songwriter and author of *S.S. Bathtub*, a book for children based on his song of the same name

> *Love is in constant potential and sometimes the mind is the last to know. But the heart may sense from across the room, from across worlds, that the beloved is approaching and the journey of another lifetime is about to begin.*
>
> ~Stephen and Ondrea Levine

Acknowledgments

One hot Austin, Texas summer in 1995, events conspired to bring the two of us together. Though totally unaware of one another's existence, we serendipitously joined a marathon training program—Austin Fit. Based on a time trial, we both were placed in the intermediate runners, a group composed of approximately thirty runners. As our group's numbers dwindled in the months preceding the race, a handful of us continued to train together at Lake Austin every Saturday morning, completing the Austin Motorola Marathon together in February 1996. And though the remaining members of our group sometimes went out for pancakes at the Magnolia Café after our weekly runs, we typically didn't see each other outside our workouts. So one Saturday we made plans to go out for music and a few beers. When the appointed time arrived, however, only two runners showed up—us (Shonnie and Bruce). And the rest, as they say, is history. We're grateful to the universe for the intersection of our paths. And we're grateful to our running buddies—Jesús, Tim, Jack, Tall Bald Larry, and Medium Bald Larry—who reneged on our planned get-together, giving us that evening all to ourselves.

I (Bruce) want to acknowledge Brad Brown and Roy Whitten, founders of the Kairos Foundation and the More To Life Program. It is through this work that I gained a sense of who I really am and my purpose in life. In addition, Shonnie and I have both benefited immensely from the relationship and sexuality workshops that this program offers. I also thank the women of my two previous marriages, both of whom helped me to learn more about myself and how to live in partnership with a significant other. My time with each of them included periods of profound love and connection along with periods of significant challenge, experiences that helped me realize that there is no one to blame, that I, and no one else, am responsible for my happiness and what I choose to make of my life.

I (Shonnie) am thankful to have had exposure to a wealth of loving relationships throughout my life. Though there were painful parts of my parents' divorce and remarriages, I learned how to open my heart to new family members while remaining faithful to my original family; find a way to move from conflict to togetherness; and be creative and flexible in building relationships that worked best for everyone involved. My early life and earlier loves enabled me to become who I am today. It is my hope that this book serves as a legacy to these people who modeled true love and helped instill in me a desire to do what's necessary to create loving, lasting, and deeply fulfilling relationships.

We want to give thanks to the folks who helped us put *I Do! I Do! The Marriage Vow Workbook* into its final form: David Lynch, Lynch Graphics, for the beautiful workbook cover design; Steve Mann, Black Box Photography, for the author photographs that capture our essence; Susan Snowden, Snowden Editorial Services, for masterfully editing the workbook in its entirety; and Heidi Costas, Workbook Goddess, for her innovative teleclass on creating workbooks that provided the initial spark for this project.

We also want to acknowledge all of those who provided us with feedback on this workbook, including Lance Secretan, Helen Bruch Pearson and Luther Smith, Allison Jordan and Gil Holmes, Ken and Elizabeth Loyd Kinnett, Howard Hanger, Bennett and Mary Page Sims, Paul Howey, David and Deanna LaMotte, Carolyn Baehr, Laurey Masterton, Sharon Parish, Fran Henry, Stewart Stokes, Barbara Brady, Jan Marie Dore, Randy Siegel, Bob and Deb Lavender, Elizabeth Pavka, Wendy Watkins, Jenny Meadows, and many others.

Finally, a special thanks to Harville Hendrix and John Hoover, who offered numerous valuable suggestions to make the workbook a more effective resource for couples who choose to use it. Their powerful support helped make this project a reality.

> *If the only prayer you said in your whole life was, "thank you," that would suffice.*
>
> ~Meister Eckhardt

Introduction

Welcome to *I Do! I Do! The Marriage Vow Workbook*. The fact that you are reading these words right now is no coincidence. You came upon this workbook because you have an intention to create a joyful and fulfilling life for yourself and a loving and lasting relationship with your partner. Be assured that you are right where you're supposed to be, doing exactly what you're supposed to be doing at this moment in time.

Some couples regard their vows as just another component of the wedding celebration, along with the bridesmaids' dresses, music selections, and reception seating. In such instances, the vows are often merely words, albeit pretty ones, to be memorized and spoken once on the special day, then likely forgotten. Not that there's anything wrong with that. But this workbook is not for them.

> *There are no accidents whatsoever in the universe.*
> ~Ram Dass

This workbook is for you and your partner . . . to help you create evocative and meaningful marriage vows that will serve you not only during the marriage ceremony itself but throughout your lives together. Whether you and your partner are conservative or liberal, whether you're straight or gay, whether this is your first marriage or you've been married previously, whether you're religious or not, you can use this workbook to create a powerful and enduring relationship.

What you'll gain from this process

As a result of reading this workbook, completing the exercises, sharing your work with your partner, and writing your marriage vows, we believe you will create a strong foundation for your relationship and enhance it in ways that you might not have imagined. In fact, working through the exercises in *The Marriage Vow Workbook* will empower you to:

- Awaken to the deepest reasons for joining your lives in marriage

- Envision what you want most from your life together

- Initiate a ritual to sustain your marriage for many years to come

- Create a loving, committed partnership that's truly ideal for both of you

The experience that led us to write this workbook

Over the years, friends and strangers alike have remarked on how we are with one another—the love we openly express, the respect that we exhibit, our ability to promptly resolve difficulties as they occur, our willingness to ask for and offer forgiveness. Probably the most important thing we did to build our fulfilling life together was to consciously create our marriage vows, the commitments we made to one another on our wedding day that we have continued to abide by. In our vow-writing process, we took the opportunity to go deep, individually and together, to gain a greater sense of who we were, why we were together, and where we wanted to go. Out of this experience, we wrote vows that brought us closer from the first instant we recited them to one another.

> *Marriage is a psychological and spiritual journey that begins in the ecstasy of attraction, meanders through a rocky stretch of self-discovery, and culminates in the creation of an intimate, joyful, lifelong union.*
>
> ~Harville Hendrix

In the years since our wedding day, we have revisited our vows on a regular basis to remind ourselves of our intentions and to return to integrity with our commitments when we've strayed. We know that we've benefited immensely from this process, and we believe that you will too.

One more thing

One of our highest intentions is to help create a world of greater compassion and connection, and this workbook was formed out of this calling. Now, by crafting your wedding vows and living them with purpose, you will be sending your love into the universe. When you take the time to open your hearts, write your truths, and share your authentic selves with one another as well as those around you, you'll not only be creating a loving, lasting marriage; you truly will, as Gandhi said, "Be the change you wish to see in the world."

We both wish you all the best, from this day forward.

Shonnie Lavender & Bruce Mulkey

Chapter 1: How to use this workbook

As you will likely discern as you read and complete the exercises in this workbook, the process you are about to undertake concerns more than just writing your marriage vows. Of course this work involves writing words of commitment for your wedding day. But more than that, there is an underlying intention to help you to form the foundation on which you can build a loving, fulfilling, lifelong relationship together. Some of the responses you provide in the exercises will be woven into your vows, while others will serve to connect you, lighten your heart, broaden your vision, and open your eyes even further to the amazing gifts you have the opportunity to share with one another.

You are welcome to use this workbook in any manner that fits best for you. To get the most from the process, however, we encourage you to create an agreement about how you will be with one another as you work through the exercises and create your marriage vows. Below are some of our recommendations.

Recommendations for completing the exercises

- Agree to fully engage in the process of creating your marriage vows and to respect one another while doing so.

- Create a supportive environment. Set aside time that will be uninterrupted and quiet so you can give your full attention to reading and completing the exercises.

- Ritualize your experience. This can be as simple as lighting a candle and putting on some relaxing music before you begin, or as elaborate as you can imagine.

- Enjoy yourself and have fun. If your mind starts to wander or you find yourself resisting this endeavor, stop for a while. Take a break. Return to the process later.

- Be gentle with yourself. If you tend to be a perfectionist or believe you must write elegant prose, give yourself permission to simply pour out your words onto paper. You can edit and rewrite later.

> *I love you, not only for what you are, but for what I am when I am with you.*
>
> ~Roy Croft

- Allow yourself as much time as you need to work through each exercise and for reflection afterwards.

- Work separately and together. First complete the exercises in each chapter on your own. By doing so you will forego the temptation to be influenced by your partner's responses. At the end of each chapter, come together and share your responses. Then proceed to the exercises in the next chapter.

- Write your responses to the exercises in the space provided with each exercise. Ideally each partner will work in his/her own workbook. However, your or your partner's responses may also be written on the worksheets at the back of this workbook or in a journal or other personal notebook. Choose the method that works best for you.

- Be completely honest with yourself and your partner. Being truthful is a vital component of all enduring relationships. Some of the exercises may prompt a conversation with your partner or some deep reflection of your own.

- Acknowledge your differences clearly and openly. Knowing how you are different from your partner is just as important as knowing how you are similar.

- Listen deeply to one another as you share this process. Listen without interrupting so you can give your partner the space to be fully heard.

- Open your heart. Your vows are already within you. You know how you want to be with your partner, what you want to create. Allow your open heart to pour forth words without self-censorship or concern about the criticism of others.

- Use language that seems natural to you. And, if you come upon a word or phrase in this workbook that feels awkward or doesn't fit your sensibilities, change it to one you prefer and move on.

- Give yourself permission to be bold. These are your vows; this is your marriage. If a particular thought or phrase truly matters to you, don't hesitate to include it.

- Take full responsibility for your experience. If there is something you want or there is something that's not working for you during the process of writing your vows, handle it and/or let your partner know without blaming or criticizing.

- Develop an agreement about your intention to get back on track if you and/or your partner get "stuck" during this process.

> *When you are for me as much as you are for yourself, and I am for you as much as I am for myself, we will start to understand the meaning of our relationship.*
>
> ~Brad Brown

What to do if you get stuck

It's possible that you and your partner will encounter some stumbling blocks or challenges as you work through the exercises in this book. Signals that you have gotten off course include:

- Resistance to the process, e.g., becoming bored, distracted, confused, anxious, frustrated, critical, or angry

- Emotional separation from your partner, e.g., feeling a lack of connection, becoming judgmental or critical, or thinking negative thoughts about him/her

If you find yourself experiencing either resistance or emotional separation, below are some techniques to help you get back on track.

1. Acknowledge what you're feeling. You might say aloud to your partner, "I feel anxious/frustrated/irritated/annoyed right now." Or "I don't feel connected to you."

2. Pause and take a few deep breaths. Recall why you're doing what you're doing. Bring an image of what you want to create together into your consciousness. Make a conscious choice to willingly reengage in the process.

3. Sometimes no words are necessary to reconnect with your partner. Look one another in the eyes; then lovingly embrace until you can feel the resistance or disconnection dissolve.

4. You may merely want a "do-over." After we experience a difference of opinion or other minor disagreement, an emotional separation will occasionally develop between us. When one of us senses this disconnection, that partner will often approach the other and gently ask, "How about a do-over?" A simple "OK" from the other and a sincere hug are usually enough to reconnect us without blame or further dialogue.

5. Take time to truly listen to each other and seek to understand your partner. Especially when you feel tension, it can be easy to make assumptions or jump to conclusions rather than giving your full attention to what your partner is actually communicating. Exercise 1-1 below will help you listen more effectively and compassionately to one another.

6. If you realize you have said or done something disrespectful or unloving that helped create an emotional disconnection with your partner, you may wish to offer a heartfelt apology for your actions and ask for forgiveness. Ideally your partner will readily accept your apology, and the disconnection is resolved. If, on the other hand, your partner has done something you find unacceptable, and you find yourself resenting him/her, we offer Exercise 1-2 below. This exercise will introduce you to a process you can use when you wish to forgive your partner (or yourself) for real or imagined insensitive actions. According to Sidney and Suzanne Simon, authors of *Forgiveness: How to Make Peace With Your Past and Get on With Your Life*, "Forgiveness is freeing up and putting to better use the energy once consumed by holding grudges, harboring resentments, and nursing unhealed wounds. It is rediscovering the strengths we always had and relocating our limitless capacity to understand and accept other people and ourselves."

7. Remember that whatever the current situation is, you have had a role in creating it. Thus, you have the power to create something different whenever you choose.

Exercise 1-1: Practicing empathic listening

Empathic listening is making a conscious effort to truly understand the other person's point of view. It's more than simply hearing the other person's words. Empathic listening involves using your eyes, heart, and gut, in addition to your ears. Empathic listening is highly effective for us when we reach an impasse with one another, but we also recommend using it for any challenging conversation. Now you have an opportunity to practice this technique.

1. Review these guidelines for effective empathic listening:

   • Enter into the conversation with an intention to truly hear and understand your partner.

   • Help your partner feel safe enough to communicate fully and honestly with you. You might express your intention to be open and to really hear what she/he has to say.

   • Listen to your partner's words with compassion and do your best to fully grasp what she/he is saying. Make an effort to put yourself in her/his situation and understand how you might have felt in similar circumstances. Let go of any need to defend yourself or refute what is being said during this time.

   • Express your compassion and openness nonverbally. Uncross your arms and legs, face your partner directly but at a distance that feels comfortable for both of you, and maintain eye contact without staring.

2. With your partner, choose a topic or issue that's ripe for discussion. Consider topics or issues that you've put off or avoided discussing.

3. Eliminate any distractions and create a quiet, safe space.

4. Choose who will be Partner A and who will be Partner B. Partner A will be the first speaker and Partner B the first listener.

> *The first duty of love is to listen.*
> *~Paul Tillich*

5. Partner A begins speaking, sharing whatever she/he wants to say about the topic at hand. Partner A can express what she/he has been feeling, believing, concerned about, etc. The purpose is to fully express the truth about the topic.

6. Partner B listens silently until Partner A has completed what she/he has to say. Then Partner B reflects back to Partner A what she/he heard. This demonstrates that Partner B is paying attention and is fully hearing what is being expressed.

7. If Partner A has a lot to say, Partner B may wait for a pause and ask to reflect back what has been said thus far.

8. At this point, if necessary, Partner A can clear up any misinterpretations by Partner B and add any additional information needed.

9. Once Partner A has completed her/his sharing and Partner B has completed reflecting these words back to Partner A, switch roles. Partner B becomes the primary speaker and Partner A is the primary listener. In these reversed roles, do steps 4 through 7 until you're both complete.

10. We consider our process complete when we both believe we've been heard and understood. Typically completion includes making choices about what we'll do or how we'll be with one another as a result of this process.

11. Using the space below record your experience of the empathic listening exercise.

<table>
<tr><td colspan="4">Empathic Listening Exercise Results</td></tr>
<tr><td colspan="4">A. Topic or issue discussed:</td></tr>
<tr><td colspan="4">B. Circle your feelings or beliefs after completing the exercise, and write any others in the spaces provided.</td></tr>
<tr><td>Connected</td><td>Heard</td><td>Understood</td><td>Better</td></tr>
<tr><td>Disconnected</td><td>Ignored</td><td>Misunderstood</td><td>Worse</td></tr>
<tr><td></td><td></td><td></td><td></td></tr>
<tr><td colspan="4">C. Write any choices or decisions you made as a result of the exercise in the space below:</td></tr>
<tr><td colspan="4"></td></tr>
<tr><td colspan="4"></td></tr>
<tr><td colspan="4"></td></tr>
</table>

Exercise 1-2: Offering forgiveness

Below is a brief process for forgiving your partner (or someone else) and addressing any resentment or bitterness you might be feeling toward him or her. During this process, remember that your resentment primarily harms you, depleting vital energy, activating self-righteousness, and disconnecting you from the loving human being that you really are. And by creating a barrier between yourself and the "perpetrator," you create a barrier between yourself and all others too.

1. Identify the person toward whom you feel resentful, and write his/her name here. Incidentally, the person toward whom you feel resentful may be you.

    _____

2. Find a comfortable place of solitude, a place where you won't be interrupted by another person, the telephone, or other electronic device.

3. Shut your eyes and take a few deep breaths down into your belly. Relax.

4. In your mind's eye, picture the person you feel resentful toward.

5. Ask yourself this question: Is holding onto my resentment worth the inner turmoil, the negative feelings, and the separation from that person and others?

6. Gain a sense of your connection with this person and make a conscious choice to release the resentment and forgive him/her. Also forgive yourself for any vengeful actions or thoughts you may have experienced.

7. As you look into the eyes of the other person in your mind's eye, tell him/her the truth of the situation; then express your love for him/her in a way that fits for you.

8. Create a new intention about how you will be and what you will do going forward in your relationship with this person. Write this intention in the space below.

    _____

    _____

    _____

    _____

9. Commit to live this new intention and do so.

Exercise 1-3: Getting what you want from this workbook

The process of creating your own unique marriage vows works best when you're clear about what you want from it. Complete statements 1 through 4 below to clarify your expectations for the work you are about to undertake, and to determine what you will do to stay on track should challenges arise. When you are done, share your responses with your partner.

1. What I want from this workbook and the process of creating our marriage vows is:

_____

_____

_____

_____

_____

2. For this process to be a success for me, it must:

_____

_____

_____

_____

3. Creating our marriage vows will be a good experience for me provided that the following things don't happen:

_____

_____

_____

_____

_____

4. Should challenges arise during the process of creating our marriage vows, I am willing to take the following actions to deal with these hurdles and complete the endeavor we've undertaken (See "What to do if you get stuck" on page 9 for suggestions.):

_____

_____

_____

_____

_____

_____

> *Really hug the person you are hugging. Make him/her very real in your arms. Breathe consciously and hug him/her with all your body, spirit and heart. If you breathe deeply like that, holding the person you love deeply like that, the energy of the care, love and mindfulness will penetrate that person and he/she will be nourished and bloom like a flower.*
>
> *~Thich Nhat Hanh*

A message for married couples who want to use this workbook

This workbook is designed for couples who want to create their own unique marriage vows—for their wedding day and beyond. But, it can also be a valuable resource for couples who are already married. Updated vows that better fit who you are as individuals and as a couple now may help to nurture and revitalize your relationship. All of the other benefits described in this workbook can be yours as well. Just turn to Chapter 1 and begin.

A message for couples who aren't planning to marry but want to create a conscious, committed relationship

After a few months of dating, we decided that we wanted to be more conscious about our relationship and our commitment to it. So together we created a document that described our intentions for how we would be with one another, a document that was actually the forerunner of the marriage vows we wrote a few years later. We know in our minds and in our hearts that having a clear purpose for our relationship at its beginning helped it to grow and flourish.

Now that the stage is set, let's look more closely at the incredible benefits you gain from writing your own marriage vows.

> *Your task is not to seek for love,*
> *but merely to seek and find all the*
> *barriers within yourself that you*
> *have built against it.*
>
> ~Rumi

Chapter 2: The benefits of writing your own marriage vows

You will notice that throughout this book we use the term "marriage vows" rather than "wedding vows." We believe that marriage vows are different from wedding vows in that marriage vows express a "lived intention," the way you will be with one another—now and through your years together—rather than words that are simply spoken once on the wedding day, then stored in the wedding photo album or the shoebox of memorabilia.

Marriage is a sacred journey, a living, evolving partnership that grows and changes each day of your life. To maintain a healthy, fulfilling marriage, a solid foundation is essential. By writing your own marriage vows, you are consciously creating this foundation. You are purposefully creating guidelines for your marriage that you intend to follow throughout your time together. As the years pass, your self-authored vows become touchstones to remind you why you made these commitments on your wonderful wedding day, why you resolved to travel this path together.

> *What happens to you in a relationship reflects far more accurately what you really want, or can tolerate, than what you keep on verbally insisting that you want.*
>
> ~Thomas Patrick Malone & Patrick Thomas Malone

By using this workbook to write your own unique marriage vows, you can strengthen your marriage in the following ways:

You're more committed. Once you've purchased this book, taken the time to complete all the exercises, and written your own marriage vows, you have already invested in your future together and expressed your deepest intentions for making this sacred commitment.

You're more connected. In sharing your deepest thoughts and feelings about your relationship with your partner as you complete the exercises in this workbook, you will increase your intimacy and deepen your connection to one another—and you're not even married yet!

You're more authentic. The marriage vows you write are a true reflection of who you really are. They are consistent with your vision, values, and beliefs. Even if you're a bit nervous on the day of your wedding, you know your vows by heart because that's the place from which they arose.

You're more creative. In writing your own vows, you send forth into the universe the vision of what you are seeking to create. By first imagining what you want in your lives together, you convert those thoughts into possibilities. When you write these possibilities down and then speak them as vows, you transform them into intentions you're committing to live by. And in sending these intentions out into the universe, you immeasurably increase the likelihood that they will become reality in your shared future.

You're more conscious. Your marriage vows have the power to support your marriage now and throughout your life with your partner. By creating a ritual to make these commitments part of your daily life, you have a greater opportunity to remain mindful of your actions in all of your relationships . . . including the one you have with yourself.

So, as you can see, there are significant benefits to writing your own marriage vows. Though it takes time, consideration, and willingness, the rewards are so profound that we believe you'll want to start your marriage in this way.

The Commitment Scale

The Commitment Scale on page 19 shows the possible levels of commitment in a relationship. The scale moves from the column on the far left, which represents a lack of commitment, to the column on the far right, which represents the deepest level of commitment. On the left, fear is the guiding motivator for action. As you move across the scale to the right, fear diminishes and love begins to flourish.

The dotted vertical line separating the two columns at the right indicates powerful similarities between a "committed" relationship and an "inspired" one. The primary distinction is that the committed couple is simply in harmony with one another while the inspired couple is conscious of a deep and abiding connection to one another and to every human, indeed every living thing. As a couple, you will likely find yourself at each of the different levels of commitment at various times in your relationship.

> *The irony of commitment is that it's deeply liberating— in work, in play, in love.*
> ~Anne Morriss

Commitment Scale

Fear ←————————————→ Love

Commitment level	1 Uncommitted	2 Obligated	3 Desiring	4 Committed	5 Inspired
What it sounds like	"I won't/can't do it!"	"I have to do it."	"I hope to do it."	"I will do it."	"Let's do it together!"
Relationship to partner	Disconnected entirely	Begrudging participation, competition, score-keeping, duty-bound	Wishing for a deeper connection in relationship	Connected to one another as allies, equals	Synergistic partnership, connection to the world-at-large
Purpose of vows	No vows or commitments	Vows as annoying rules	Vows as expressions of how you hope you and your partner can be	Vows as commitments consciously chosen and willingly followed	Vows as part of who you are, lived naturally with little conscious effort
Prevalent feelings	Isolation, hopelessness, resistance	Resentment, impatience, frustration, irritation	Anxiety, longing, expectant	Happiness, satisfaction, contentment	Love, joy, gratitude, fulfillment

Exercise 2-1: How committed are you?

Determine your level of commitment in your relationship by completing the exercise below.

1. Review the Commitment Scale on page 19 and write your level of commitment in your relationship in the space below:

   _____

2. Are you at the level of commitment that's ideal for you and for the marriage you want to create? Why or why not?

   _____

   _____

   _____

   _____

3. How do you think that working through the exercises in this workbook will sustain or increase your level of commitment?

   _____

   _____

   _____

Another way you can use the Commitment Scale is to "take your temperature" from time to time and assess whether you're connected to your partner in the way you want to be. You might even use the scale once you've written your vows to see how committed you are to living each vow you've chosen. Additionally, you can add your own examples to the scale so that you'll have reminders of what you say and do when you're at one of these levels.

Now that you've warmed up with these exercises, you'll begin laying the foundation for your married life. Let's start by celebrating what you love about your partner, the strengths you each bring to your relationship, and the reasons you've decided to join your lives in marriage.

> Passion is the quickest to develop, and the quickest to fade. Intimacy develops more slowly, and commitment more gradually still.
> ~Robert Sternberg

Chapter 3: Articulating your appreciation for one another

You are about to start your married life with the person of your dreams. Most likely, your heart is filled with joy and you're envisioning a long and extraordinary life together. This chapter is designed to make you even more conscious of the reasons you have chosen to fully commit to one another, as well as to provide you with a touchstone as you go forward in your relationship. Some of what you write in the following exercises may provide you with words of praise and love to include in your marriage vows. But more than that, what you discover can be accessed in years to come to heal a breach in your relationship or reconnect you with your partner. This may be especially helpful during times when you find yourself focusing more on faults and imperfections than what attracted you to one another in the first place.

You may wish to review the recommendations for doing the exercises in this workbook on pages 8 and 9 before you begin. Please note that every exercise provides space for you to write your responses. There are worksheets in the back of this book that you may also use. After completing the exercises in this chapter, meet with your partner to share your responses and discuss what they might mean for your relationship.

> *A friend is someone who knows the song in your heart and can sing it back to you when you have forgotten the words.*
>
> ~Unknown

Exercise 3-1: What makes your partner the right one for you?

In this exercise, you will answer questions that will help you become more conscious of the reasons you have chosen to be in a committed relationship with one another. For each question, write out your answers in the space provided.

1. I have chosen to be in a lifelong, fully committed relationship with my partner because . . .

_____

_____

_____

_____

_____

_____

_____

_____

_____

_____

_____

2. Ways my partner seems to complete me are . . .

_____

_____

_____

_____

_____

_____

_____

_____

_____

_____

_____

_____

_____

3. The five things I love most about my partner are . . .

_____

_____

_____

_____

_____

_____

_____

_____

_____

_____

_____

_____

Exercise 3-2: What strengths do you each bring to the relationship?

Each of you has positive attributes or strengths that affect how you relate to others. Below is a list of some possible strengths. On the following pages you will be asked to choose which of these strengths you possess and which you believe your partner possesses.

Strengths				
accepting	acknowledging	adventurous	athletic	attractive
authentic	bold	calm	cautious	championing
common sense	compassionate	courageous	creative	curious
dependable	detail-oriented	discerning	emotionally intelligent	encouraging
energetic	enthusiastic	fair	forgiving	generous
gentle	graceful	helpful	honest	humorous
inspiring	intelligent	intuitive	leading	light-hearted
loving	loyal	nonjudgmental	nurturing	open-minded
organized	passionate	patient	physically strong	planning
playful	resilient	risk taking	sexual	spiritual
spontaneous	supportive	tasteful	tender	trusting
trustworthy	vulnerable	visionary	warm	wise

Marriage is not just spiritual communion, it is also remembering to take out the trash.

~Joyce Brothers

1. In the spaces provided below, write at least eight strengths that best describe **you**. Refer to the list on page 14 to make your choices. Then prioritize your strengths one through eight, with one as your greatest strength.

   My strengths are . . .

   _____

   _____

   _____

   _____

   _____

   _____

   _____

   _____

   _____

   _____

   _____

   _____

2. In the spaces provided below, write at least eight strengths that best describe **your partner**. Refer to the list on page 14 to make your choices. Then prioritize her/his strengths one through eight, with one as her/his greatest strength.

My partner's strengths are . . .

_____

_____

_____

_____

_____

_____

_____

_____

_____

_____

_____

3. In the spaces provided below, write the strengths your partner possesses that complement your weaknesses. Example: Your partner has the strength of being organized while you have the weakness of being disorganized.

    My partner's strengths and my weaknesses they complement are . . .

    _____

    _____

    _____

    _____

    _____

    _____

    _____

    _____

    _____

    _____

    _____

We hope that the exercises in this chapter provide you greater clarity regarding why you have chosen one another, why you have decided to enter into this momentous commitment called marriage. You may or may not decide to use your responses to the exercises in this chapter as part of your marriage vows. Nonetheless, the knowledge you've gained about one another can serve you well throughout your lives together. For as much as you love one another, there will be times when you lose touch with what is special about your partner, why you chose to be together in this way. In those instances (and others), you can return to these pages and read what you've written to help rekindle those magical feelings about one another and reconnect to the truth about who you are.

Now that you've gained some insights regarding what you appreciate about one another, let's go to Chapter 4 and the opportunity to share thoughts and feelings about what you want for yourself and the relationship that sometimes go unspoken.

> *We often unconsciously find in our partners the parts of us that are undeveloped. The other somehow seems to complete us. But that which may attract us to a significant other can become one of our greatest challenges once we've been in the relationship for a while.*
>
> ~John Hoover

Chapter 4: Sharing what you want for yourself and the relationship

Even if you've been dating for some time or have already made a deep commitment to one another, publicly proclaiming your marriage vows—to one another, to those close to you, to your community—begins a new phase in your relationship. The exercises in this chapter provide an opportunity to be clear with one another regarding what it is you each want, and even expect, from your marriage and from each other. Your responses may become a part of your vows should you wish to articulate how you'll be with one another, how you'll comfort and love one another, and how you'll offer support. In addition, you may choose to consider your responses as a contour map of your deepest wants and desires, a guide to help your partner know and understand you better—shortcuts to your satisfaction, detours around your dramas, and important landmarks of your inner landscape.

You may wish to review the recommendations for doing the exercises in this workbook on pages 8 and 9 before you begin. Please note that every exercise provides space for you to write your responses. In addition, there are worksheets in the back of this book that you may use. After completing the exercises in this chapter, meet with your partner to share your responses and discuss what they might mean for your relationship.

> *Whatever we expect with confidence becomes our own self-fulfilling prophecy.*
>
> ~Brian Tracy

Exercise 4-1: How do you want to receive love and support?

It's important to remove any barriers to love in your relationship. Rather than expecting your partner to read your mind, it's invaluable to tell her/him what you're thinking. In Exercise 4-1, write down the precise ways in which you best receive love and support so your partner's love will have the best opportunity to reach you unhindered. Several of these ideas were drawn from the work of Gary Chapman in his book *The Five Love Languages*.

1. I feel loved, appreciated, or affirmed when my partner says . . .

_____

_____

_____

_____

_____

_____

_____

_____

_____

_____

2. Acts of compassion and kindness my partner could do for me include . . .

_____

_____

_____

_____

_____

_____

_____

_____

_____

_____

_____

_____

_____

3. Ways I like to be physically touched are . . .

_____

_____

_____

_____

_____

_____

_____

_____

_____

_____

_____

_____

_____

4. Quality time with my partner includes such activities as . . .

_____

_____

_____

_____

_____

_____

_____

_____

_____

_____

_____

_____

_____

5. Types of gifts (material, emotional, spiritual, etc.) I enjoy receiving are . . .

_____

_____

_____

_____

_____

_____

_____

_____

_____

_____

_____

Exercise 4-2: What do you want when you're not at your best?

As with all relationships, there will be times in your marriage when life is challenging. This exercise will help you better understand how to be with one another during times of discontent, disagreement, and disappointment.

1. It's easy for me to get annoyed, moody, angry, or otherwise out of sorts when these things happen (Note: These could be certain behaviors by your partner, difficult circumstances at work, or other challenging situations.):

_____

_____

_____

_____

_____

_____

_____

_____

_____

_____

_____

2. When I'm annoyed, moody, angry, or otherwise out of sorts about something, I behave in the following ways:

_____

_____

_____

_____

_____

_____

_____

_____

_____

_____

_____

_____

3. The best way for my partner to respond to me when I'm annoyed, moody, angry, or otherwise out of sorts about something is . . .

_____

_____

_____

_____

_____

_____

_____

_____

_____

_____

_____

_____

4. It's best if my partner avoids doing or saying the following when I'm annoyed, moody, angry, or otherwise out of sorts about something:

_____

_____

_____

_____

_____

_____

_____

_____

_____

_____

_____

_____

Exercise 4-3: What's working in your relationship? What's not?

This exercise will give you an excellent sense of the areas in your relationship that are working well and the areas in which you would like to create something different.

Rating your relationship				
Using this table, rate each of the areas of your relationship on a scale of 1 through 5, with 5 being the ideal amount.				
	Too little	**Almost enough**		**Just right**
Authenticity	1	2	3	4	5
Commitment	1	2	3	4	5
Communication	1	2	3	4	5
Community	1	2	3	4	5
Connection	1	2	3	4	5
Financial security	1	2	3	4	5
Forgiveness	1	2	3	4	5
Home as sanctuary	1	2	3	4	5
Honesty	1	2	3	4	5
Integrity	1	2	3	4	5
Intimacy	1	2	3	4	5
Joy	1	2	3	4	5
Mutual support	1	2	3	4	5
Personal growth	1	2	3	4	5
Physical activities	1	2	3	4	5
Playfulness	1	2	3	4	5
Service to others	1	2	3	4	5
Sexuality	1	2	3	4	5
Spirituality	1	2	3	4	5
Trust	1	2	3	4	5

1. From the table above, select the three areas of your relationship that you're most satisfied with.

_____

_____

_____

_____

2. From the table above, select the three areas of your relationship that you're least satisfied with.

_____

_____

_____

_____

3. With your partner choose the one area of your relationship that you both commit to improve. Write it in the space below along with initial steps you will take.

_____

_____

_____

_____

_____

Congratulations! You have now clarified your wants and expectations for your marriage and have made them known to your partner. It is important to keep in mind that these are not demands that *should* be fulfilled, but requests to be fulfilled if your partner is willing. Of course, just because you each have a more detailed picture of what you want to receive from your partner doesn't mean there won't be issues to discuss and compromises to make. However, you will begin your marriage better prepared in this regard than many couples.

So on to the next step, confirming your convictions—the values, issues, and goals that are most important to you.

> *The most beautiful thing about love—and the most difficult—is that it makes us go back to our unfinished places and relationships and, maybe, finish them. Your partner is the person who helps you do that, not by serving you, but by serving as a mirror for you, by his or her honesty.*
>
> ~Stephen Levine

Chapter 5: Confirming your convictions

In a marriage, although you are still two distinct human beings, a portion of your life is truly linked to your partner. It is important to have both clarity and congruence with your partner on the values that influence you, the causes for which you have the most passion, and the goals toward which you will strive. The exercises in this chapter are designed to help you do just that. Remember, even though you may not have all the same values, causes, and goals, being conscious of them will better enable you to make choices that fit for you individually and as a couple. You may decide to express the information from this chapter in your vows, perhaps making commitments about what you stand for or believe in. This material may also be useful in completing the exercises in Chapter 6 when you write your vision for your marriage.

You may wish to review the recommendations for doing the exercises in this workbook on pages 8 and 9 before you begin. Please note that every exercise provides space for you to write your responses. In addition, there are worksheets in the back of this book that you may also use. After completing the exercises in this chapter, meet with your partner to share your responses and discuss what they might mean for your relationship.

Exercise 5-1: What values do you stand for?

A value is a principle, standard, or quality considered valuable or desirable. While your personal values need not all be the same as your partner's, it is important for you to know what your personal values are and which values you share. Below and on the next page is a list of common values. You may add others in the spaces provided.

Values				
abundance	accomplishment	acquisition	attraction	authenticity
awakening	boldness	change	collaboration	commitment
communication	community	compassion	connection	consciousness
conservation	contribution	cooperation	courage	creativity
democracy	detachment	devotion	discernment	discipline
elegance	empathy	encouragement	energetic	enlightenment
equality	excellence	excitement	fairness	faith
family	following calling	forgiveness	fostering	freedom

friendship	fulfilling my life mission	fun	generosity	grace
gratitude	hard work	harmony	honesty	honor
humility	impeccability	independence	ingenuity	innovation
inspiration	integrity	intensity	intimacy	joy
justice	knowledge	leadership	listening	love
loyalty	material wealth	meaningful work	nourishment	oneness
openness	originality	partnership	passion	patriotism
peace	personal growth	pleasure	power	practicality
privacy	problem solving	prosperity	quest	religion
respect	risk	safety	security	self-reliance
sensitivity	sensuality	service	sexuality	sharing my unique gifts
silence	simplicity	spirituality	spontaneity	strength
sustainability	teamwork	tolerance	tradition	trust
truth	unity	vision	wisdom	

We can tell our values by looking at our checkbook stubs.

~Gloria Steinem

1. From the list on pages 44 and 45 put a checkmark next to all the values that are important to you.

2. From the values you selected in item number 1 above, choose your five most essential values. Write them below in order of descending importance.

_____

_____

_____

_____

_____

3. The essential values that I share with my partner are . . .

_____

_____

_____

_____

_____

Exercise 5-2: What issues and causes are most important to you?

In this exercise, you have the opportunity to identify issues you stand for as a couple. Knowing what causes inspire you and compel you to act is both practical (helping you decide what charities you'll support or where you'll volunteer your time) and spiritual (empowering you to work together for a greater purpose).

Issues and Causes		
Below are various issues and causes that may be important to you and your partner. You may add other issues and causes in the spaces provided.		
animal welfare	arms control	children's welfare
democracy	disease prevention	education
energy conservation	environment	fair trade
family values	free speech & media	gay rights
globalization	government reform	gun control
healthy food	homelessness	human rights
hunger	immigration	justice
mental health	natural disaster response	peace
population growth	poverty	racial equality
religious freedom	spirituality	universal health care
war on terror	women's rights	workers' rights

> *The place God calls you to is the place where your deep gladness and the world's deep hunger meet.*
>
> ~Frederick Buechner

1. My top three issues and causes are . . .

_____

_____

_____

_____

_____

_____

2. The issues and causes we share as a couple are . . .

_____

_____

_____

_____

_____

_____

Exercise 5-3: What goals do you want to achieve together?

It's likely that you and your partner will share some goals and not others. It is therefore a valuable exercise to identify your personal goals, the goals your partner has, and the goals that are important to both of you.

Now take time to review your answers for Exercises 5-1 and 5-2 and determine what goals you wish to set for yourself and your relationship.

1. My four most important goals are (e.g., have children, serve the community, build financial security, travel abroad, follow my calling, live a simple life) . . .

_____

_____

_____

_____

_____

_____

_____

_____

_____

_____

_____

2. The goals that I share with my partner are . . .

_____

_____

_____

_____

_____

_____

_____

_____

_____

_____

Now you have a greater sense of the purpose for your life together, the values that guide you, and the goals that are most important to you. This information will be invaluable as you begin the next chapter; in it you will be guided to write a joint vision for your marriage—a compelling picture of where you want to go together.

Chapter 6: Creating a joint vision

In this chapter you will create a vision—a vivid mental image—for the future of your marriage. When you create a powerful vision for yourselves, it can support you in the following ways:

- A powerful vision has an excellent chance of becoming reality.

- A vision helps you make choices that truly fit for you.

- A vision can inspire you to overcome the challenges that you confront.

> *If you don't have a dream, how are you going to have a dream come true?*
> ~Walt Disney

Once completed, you may incorporate your vision (or an element of it) into your marriage vows if you so choose. Below we share the vision that guides our lives together as an example of a joint vision.

> **Bruce and Shonnie's vision**
>
> *We are conscious, connected, loving, and present in the moment. We follow our true callings and do so with great passion. We attract all of the resources we need to live prosperous and fulfilling lives almost effortlessly. The way we use our time and our other resources is congruent with who we really are and our deepest values. We take time for doing and being—together and with others; the balance of these elements is ideal for us. We are strong, healthy, vibrant, and active. Our relationship continues to deepen, becoming even more supportive, loving, and fulfilling. We feel the mystery of life and acknowledge our place in it. We express profound gratitude for the present moment and for the fullness of our lives.*

You may wish to review the recommendations for doing the exercises in this workbook on pages 8 and 9 before you begin. Please note that every exercise provides space for you to write your responses. In addition, there are worksheets in the back of this book that you may also use. After completing the exercises in this chapter, meet with your partner to share your responses and discuss what they might mean for your relationship.

Exercise 6-1: Creating a vision for your marriage

Through the following short visualizations, you'll have the opportunity to picture the future you want to experience with your partner. Once imagined, you then have the power to create what you've seen first in your mind's eye.

An enjoyable way to do this exercise is for one partner to guide the other through the visualization (steps 1-9 below). For instance, Partner B slowly reads all the text in steps 1-9, allowing Partner A to relax and experience the visualization. Partner B may even volunteer to write down what Partner A says at the completion of each visualization. After the writing is done for step 9 and Partner A has finished, switch roles and have Partner A slowly read the instructions and write notes as Partner B enjoys her/his own visualization.

A word of caution: If you think that guiding one another through the visualization would hinder your experience of the process in any way (self-censorship, pleasing your partner by following his/her lead, saying the "right" thing, etc.), do it solo instead.

1. Create a quiet, peaceful environment for yourself. You may want to light a candle or play some soft relaxing music.

2. Loosen or remove any constricting clothing (belt, tight pants, etc.). Find a comfortable place to sit—firm but yielding.

3. Close your eyes and take three deep, full breaths, inhaling through your nose and exhaling through your mouth.

4. As you breathe out, let your body relax.

5. Think of a time when you were feeling deep love for your partner. Reexperience what you saw, what you heard, what you were feeling, and bask in the glow of this memory for one to two minutes. Write a few sentences describing what you've just experienced.

_____

_____

_____

_____

6. Now visualize you and your partner five years from now living a life that's ideal for both of you. Where are you? What are you doing? How has your relationship changed? What have you achieved? How are you living your lives—as individuals and as a couple? Simply notice the pictures and sensations you experience for a few minutes. Now write a few sentences expressing what you've just experienced.

_____

_____

_____

_____

_____

_____

_____

_____

_____

_____

_____

7. Next visualize you and your partner ten years from now still living a life that's ideal for you. Where are you? What are you doing? How has your relationship changed? What have you achieved? How are you living your lives—as individuals and as a couple? After a few minutes, write a few sentences expressing what you've just experienced.

_____

_____

_____

_____

_____

_____

_____

_____

_____

_____

_____

_____

8. Finally visualize yourself lying in bed, knowing that your time in the bodily form is almost complete, your death is at hand. What is your partner saying to you? What are you saying in return? What do you most want her/him to know? Now write a few sentences expressing what you've just experienced.

_____

_____

_____

_____

_____

_____

_____

_____

_____

_____

_____

_____

9. In the space below, write any final thoughts or feelings from these visualizations that you have not yet expressed.

_____

_____

_____

_____

_____

_____

_____

_____

_____

_____

_____

_____

_____

10. After considering each of your visualizations above, craft a joint vision for your relationship—where the two of you want to be, what you will create together during your lifetime. You may want to begin with a vision for your first five or ten years together.

_____

_____

_____

_____

_____

_____

_____

_____

_____

_____

_____

_____

Congratulations! You've completed the foundational work for writing your marriage vows. You've recalled what you love about each other and why you're so well-suited for one another. You've clearly identified what you want and need from your partner. You've clarified the goals that are most important in your lives and identified the values that will guide you in the years ahead. You've seen in your mind's eye a clear and compelling vision for your life together as a couple. You are now ready to put pen to paper, taking the insights and understanding you now have, and craft marriage vows that truly fit who you are and what you intend to create in your life together.

> *An enlightened marriage is a commitment to participate in the process of mutual growth and forgiveness, sharing a common goal of service to God.*
>
> ~Marianne Williamson

Chapter 7: Writing your vows

In Chapters 2 through 6, you put the groundwork in place for your marriage vows. It is now time to use your minds and hearts to choose the commitments you will make to one another for your life together. As you write, remember the purpose and nature of vows as described in Chapter 2.

Below is a suggested process for distilling what you've written in the preceding exercises into marriage vows that you want to share on your wedding day and commit to for all your days together. If you each plan to use the same vows, you may want to complete the exercises in this chapter together. If you have chosen to write unique vows for each of you, you will do the following exercises individually. You then have the option of sharing your vows with your partner before your wedding day or keeping them as a special gift that you offer for the first time during the wedding ceremony itself. Regardless of whether you write joint or individual vows, take time to go deep with these questions and continue to be sincere and openhearted in your responses.

> Vow: *a solemn pledge to oneself or to another or to a deity to do something or to behave in a certain manner*

You may wish to review the recommendations for doing the exercises in this workbook on pages 8 and 9 before you begin. Please note that every exercise provides space for you to write your responses. In addition, there are worksheets in the back of this book that you may also use. After completing the exercises in this chapter, meet with your partner to share your responses and discuss what they might mean for your relationship.

Exercise 7-1: Getting personal

In this section you will be reviewing some of the earlier exercises and bringing forward the information and ideas that you want to weave into your actual vows.

1. How do you intend to write your vows? Possibilities include (1) writing them together, with each partner using the same vows; (2) writing them separately with unique vows for each partner; or (3) a variation of the two. Write your preference in the space provided below.

_____

_____

2. Review Exercise 2-1 in Chapter 2. Do you want to include anything about your level of commitment to your relationship in your vows? If so, write it in the space below.

_____

_____

_____

_____

_____

_____

_____

_____

_____

_____

_____

_____

_____

3. Review Exercises 3-1 and 3-2 in Chapter 3. Do you want to include any of the reasons you are in this relationship in your marriage vows? If so, write them in the space below.

_____

_____

_____

_____

_____

_____

_____

_____

_____

_____

_____

_____

4. Review Exercises 4-1 through 4-3 in Chapter 4. Do you want to include any of the things you want for yourself and your relationship in your vows? If so, write them in the space below.

_____

_____

_____

_____

_____

_____

_____

_____

_____

_____

_____

_____

5. Review exercises 5-1 through 5-3 in Chapter 5. Do you want to include any of your values, important issues and causes, or goals you want to achieve in your vows? If so, write them in the space below.

_____

_____

_____

_____

_____

_____

_____

_____

_____

_____

_____

_____

_____

_____

6. Review exercise 6-1 in Chapter 6. Do you want to include any of the elements of your vision for your marriage in your vows? If so, write them in the space below.

_____

_____

_____

_____

_____

_____

_____

_____

_____

_____

_____

7. Do you have a favorite poem, song lyric, holy reading, or quote that you want to use in your vows? If so, write it in the space below.

_____

_____

_____

_____

_____

_____

_____

_____

_____

_____

_____

_____

_____

8. If your partner remembered only one thing from your vows, what would you want it to be?

_____

_____

_____

_____

_____

_____

_____

_____

_____

_____

_____

_____

_____

9. What are some powerful, evocative words that you want to use in your vows? You might consider *love, compassion, respect, cherish, honor, commit, trust, acknowledge, forgiveness, esteem, intention, vision* and *support*, among others.

_____

_____

_____

_____

_____

_____

_____

_____

_____

_____

_____

10. What other thoughts, feelings, or images do you want to express in your vows?

_____

_____

_____

_____

_____

_____

_____

_____

Tips to remember when writing your vows

Here are a few things to consider as you write your marriage vows in Exercise 7-2:

- Do you intend to share your vows with your partner before the wedding ceremony or will they be a surprise? If you want them to be a surprise, choose a trusted loved one to run them by.

- Write vows in the positive (e.g., "I will treat you with respect," instead of, "I will not be disrespectful toward you.").

- Write vows in the way you speak. If you're plainspoken, write your vows that way and leave flowery prose to others.

- Write vows that register a strong "yes" within you when you read them to yourself. Something inside you will let you know that this commitment is right for you.

- Write vows that speak to the best in you and your partner.

- Write vows that have a sense of the sacred. Such vows come from deep within and you will willingly take them on. If a vow seems to be a directive, a command, or an ultimatum, set it aside and choose another.

- Write vows that are broad enough to apply to your life today and your life fifty years from now.

- Write vows that make you feel joyful, inspired, excited, and optimistic.

- Write vows using bold language. Examples include "I will," "I commit to," "As your partner/husband/wife/friend/lover I intend to . . ."

- Write vows that matter to you and your partner, that authentically express what's in your heart. Your vows are for the two of you, though you may wish to ask your family and/or your community to support you in keeping them.

- You may wish to include some vows for your immediate family or your community of friends. For example, you may want to ask your parents to accept your partner as part of their family, or ask friends to support both of you in keeping your marriage vows.

> *The most beautiful and romantic relationship has to begin with you. You are responsible for one half of the relationship: your half. When you respect yourself, you respect your beloved. When you honor yourself, you honor your beloved.*
>
> ~don Miguel Ruiz

- Write your vows in language that your family and guests will be able to understand. Inside jokes are OK, but only if most others will comprehend the general idea of what you are saying.

- Once written, read your vows aloud to make sure the language flows well; revise any awkward sections or phrases that you might stumble on.

- Do a run-through before the wedding day to get comfortable saying your vows.

- If you intend to memorize your vows, keep a copy of them with you during the ceremony, just in case. Or have the officiant lead you through them, with the officiant saying them first and you repeating them afterward.

- Coordinate your efforts with your officiant. Remember that some religions have restrictions on the vows that can be used in a marriage ceremony. Your officiant may be able to offer suggestions for your vows and incorporate them seamlessly into the ceremony.

Exercise 7-2: Writing your marriage vows

OK! The time has come to write your marriage vows. Use the space below to write a draft version of your vows. Refer to your responses to the questions in Exercise 7-1, in addition to other notes or material that you want to incorporate. Turn off your internal editor, that critical inner voice, and let your feelings and thoughts pour out onto the paper. You can type them up and edit them later. Below is an example of marriage vows—our own from our May 30, 1999 wedding.

Bruce to Shonnie

I will join you in full partnership to cocreate the life we both envision.

I will join you in living consciously, purposefully, passionately, congruently.

I will join you in creating true community and a more compassionate world in which to live.

I will laugh and dance and sing and have fun with you.

I will tell you the truth even when I think you might not want to hear it, and I will hear you when you tell me your truth.

I will afford you your humanity and not expect you to always be at your best.

When you forget who you really are, I'll remind you of your power, spirit, integrity, intelligence, creativity, athleticism, and beauty.

I will remember that any anger, resentment, frustration I show toward you is more about me than about you and will refuse to hold ill will toward you.

I will be true to you and honor the commitments that we make to one another for all our days. I will open my heart to you and love you with all my being.

Shonnie to Bruce

I will be authentically me. Bringing all my gifts and challenges and willingly using all the tools I have to fully live out my life's purpose.

I will be your mirror. Reflecting the truth and reminding you of who you are, listening attentively with an open heart and mind as I seek to better understand and support you in fully living your life's purpose.

I will be your helpmate. Willingly sharing our responsibilities and honors, owning my part in creating our life, readily and fully forgiving, and working together to put us back on course when we stray from our path.

I will be your partner. Treating you with respect and equality, being creative and flexible in living interdependently in a way that reflects who we are individually and as a couple.

I will be your lover. Passionate and playful, tender and loyal, sharing myself fully and nurturing our love so that we grow ever more intimate.

I will be your friend. Honest and trustworthy, compassionate and committed, sharing all that life brings us.

I will be your companion. Honoring these sacred vows as we walk together, hand in hand, heart to heart, soul to soul, for all our days, giving all that we have and being all that we are, to create a world full of peace, love, and understanding.

Now use the space below to write your marriage vows.

_____

_____

_____

_____

_____

_____

_____

_____

_____

_____

_____

_____

_____

_____

_____

_____

_____

_____

_____

_____

_____

_____

_____

_____

Congratulations! You've written marriage vows that are ideal for you! Even if you make revisions, you've done the majority of the work. Be sure to take time to celebrate your achievement with your partner, and acknowledge yourselves for the amazing creation you now hold in your hands! Below are a few notes to consider once you're ready to polish your vows for their final state.

How you'll know your vows are ideal for you

There are no "right" or "perfect" vows for marriage. The commitments you make are unique to who you are, what you value, and what you want to create in your lives. Your vows may be different from the ones your partner decides to make, they may be similar, or they may be identical. Your vows are a reflection of you and, together with your partner's vows, a representation of what you'll stand for as a married couple.

To determine if the vows you've written are ideal for you, consider the following questions and check the box if the answer is "yes." Do your vows . . .

- ☐ warm your heart when you read them, and truthfully represent what you want to create together?

- ☐ characterize lofty yet attainable goals that reflect your deepest values?

- ☐ inspire you to commit to them out of pure choice (rather than something you "should" do)?

- ☐ speak the truth about who each of you really are and how you want to be with one another?

- ☐ express your willingness to be cocreators of your marriage, each taking full responsibility for his/her part?

- ☐ call you to give your absolute best in your relationship, yet allow you the freedom to be yourself and, being human, sometimes fall short?

- ☐ imbue you with joy when you think of living together with the daily intention of fulfilling your commitments to one another to the best of your ability?

Let your hearts inform you as you read your vows. This process is more about drawing forth your intuitive and emotional wisdom than it is about crafting some grammatically perfect, smooth-sounding sentences. If the vows uplift your spirit, move you to say "yes, yes, yes," and draw forth a broad smile, you've got vows that matter to you and add strength to your life as a couple.

> *I define love as the place where my heart touches your heart and adds to who we both are as persons.*
>
> ~Lance Secretan

Now that your marriage vows are written, it's time to create a ritual that will support you to keep them throughout your lives together.

Chapter 8: Living your vows

Using your vows beyond your wedding day

Most couples practice their vows for the wedding, recite them on the wedding day, and then go about living their lives without revisiting them again. We believe that marriage vows are sacred promises we make to one another for all of our days together. And we believe it's important that they continue to serve as touchstones—reminders of who we are, why we're together, and where we want to go.

When used in this manner, your vows act as your relationship compass—a tool to keep you moving in the direction that you envision for your marriage. By regularly revisiting your vows, you make it easier to change course when you find yourself headed in an unintended direction. If, for instance, I (Shonnie) read my vow, "I will be your partner. Treating you with respect and equality . . ." and realize that I've been withholding information about our finances (a role I'm responsible for in my marriage), then I can say that I've not kept this vow because I don't view withholding information as a respectful behavior. In that very moment of rereading the vow and realizing my misstep, I can acknowledge it and recommit to my vow to treat Bruce with respect and equality. Such action restores me to integrity with my word, builds trust, and reunites us as I reaffirm my stand for how I will be with him in our marriage.

> *You have the power to create. Your power is so strong that whatever you believe comes true.*
>
> ~don Miguel Ruiz

Suggestions for using your vows to strengthen your marriage

In order for your vows to help strengthen your marriage, you'll need to revisit them frequently to reconnect with your intentions, your inner wisdom, and your partner. Use this time to listen to your partner, tell your truth, and deepen the connection you already have. Below are our suggestions for how to experience the profound benefits of a relationship reconnection ritual.

- Review your vows at least monthly.

- Read them aloud to each other, taking time to look into your partner's eyes. This can be one of the most connecting and loving actions you take with each other.

- Remind yourself that the vows you wrote are as much for your benefit as they are for your partner's. They are reminders of how you want to be in this relationship.

- Make recommitting to your vows part of a larger relationship-deepening practice. We reread our vows at the beginning of our relationship meeting (see "Our personal practice" below).

- Keep your vows visible. Both of us have copies in our day-planners. We had our original relationship commitments (the vows we created when we were dating) printed in calligraphy onto poster board so we could see them every day and appreciate their meaning and uniqueness.

- Acknowledge yourself for having fulfilled your vows as best you could. Even if you've fallen short of your commitments, give yourself credit for what you have done.

- Be gentle with each other as you use your vows to strengthen your marriage.

- Remember to bring love and compassion into the process along with your introspection and honesty.

Recognize that revisiting and recommitting to your vows is not about being "right" or "wrong." It is simply an opportunity to check in and see if you're fulfilling the promises you made on your wedding day and to change course if you've strayed from your intention.

Our personal practice

We meet at least monthly and focus specifically on our relationship. We have a regular schedule in which we plan for 30-60 minutes of uninterrupted time (phones turned off, computer monitors dimmed, etc.). We generally light a candle and put on soft instrumental music in the background. When we first sit down, we take time to breathe and relax so that we can be fully present with each other. Here is the structure of our meeting:

> *Do acts of kindness, love, and generosity every day, even when you are not in the mood.*
>
> *~Michael Lerner*

1. We reread our vows aloud to one another, looking into each other's eyes as we did on our wedding day.

2. We then verbally acknowledge each other for ways of being and things accomplished that we've noticed since our last meeting (e.g., anything from appreciating Bruce for cleaning the kitchen or being a loving son and calling his mom twice a week, to acknowledging Shonnie for keeping the house quiet so Bruce could sleep in on Saturday or for her willingness to do additional volunteer work at our church).

3. Next we tell the truth about any thoughts or feelings that have gone unspoken since we last met. Whether we were actually withholding information or were just unaware we had something to share, this is a time to make a clean breast of it.

4. As needed, we recommit to any vows we haven't fulfilled. For instance, if Bruce is recommitting, he speaks the vow aloud, shares how he believes he missed the mark (without guilt, shame, or excuses), and then recommits to keeping the vow.

5. Finally, we handle some practical issues. We review our schedules for the upcoming week so we can coordinate them when necessary. Sometimes we look at our budget and evaluate our spending for the previous month.

We complete our meeting in a loving way—by kissing, snuggling quietly, looking into each other's eyes, dancing to a favorite song, or whatever lets us close this time purposefully and in a connected way.

Exercise 8-1: Design your own marriage vow support system

Sit down with your partner after reviewing the information above and complete the following worksheet together.

1. We are willing to commit to a regular meeting as part of our marriage vow support system because . . .

_____

_____

_____

_____

2. We will meet to review our vows and strengthen our marriage (weekly, monthly, etc.) . . .

_____

_____

_____

_____

3. We will meet at the following times on the following dates: (Block out these days/times on your calendars for the next year right now.)

_____

_____

_____

4. We will set the stage for our meeting (e.g., music, reading a prayer at the beginning, silently sitting and looking into each other's eyes) in the following manner:

_____

_____

_____

_____

_____

_____

_____

_____

5. We will structure our meeting as follows: (See "Our personal practice" outline above for ideas.)

_____

_____

_____

_____

_____

_____

_____

_____

_____

_____

_____

6. We will also do the following things to keep our marriage vows alive (e.g., posting the vows in a prominent location, reading a vow to each other before bedtime each night, sharing vows with our coach or therapist and asking for his/her support in keeping the commitments):

_____

_____

_____

_____

_____

_____

_____

_____

_____

_____

Marriage Vow Pledge

Now that you've created a Marriage Vow Support System, we invite you to confirm your commitment to the practice of living your vows by agreeing to and signing the Marriage Vow Pledge on the next page. We recommend that you hang a copy of the pledge and your marriage vows where you'll see them every day.

MARRIAGE VOW PLEDGE

Our marriage vows are sacred commitments that we will abide by throughout our lives together. We will meet regularly to uphold our marriage vows, deepen our connection, and strengthen our relationship. We will post this pledge and our marriage vows in a prominent place in our home to remind of us of our deep and abiding commitment and our love for one another.

_____	_____
Signature	Signature
_____	_____
Date	Date

Dance like no one is watching,

Love like you'll never be hurt,

Sing like no one is listening,

Live like it's heaven on earth

~William Purkey

Congratulations on your willingness to sign this pledge. Before you return to planning the other aspects of your wedding, let us offer a few closing thoughts and wishes.

Chapter 9: Some final thoughts

You have embarked upon a magical journey, the path of which lies before you. By choosing to consciously compose your own unique marriage vows, we believe that you have established a solid foundation for your life together. These loving commitments will serve you well, in good times and in those that are challenging.

We deeply acknowledge you for the thoughtfulness of the actions you have taken in completing the tasks in the preceding chapters of this workbook. Such actions are rare in today's society and signify the depth of your love and loyalty for one another and your intention for a fulfilling and lasting partnership.

We are honored to have played a part in the creation of your vows to one another. As our final contribution in this workbook, we offer this blessing from the Apache Indian tradition as our wish for your life together from this day forward.

> *Now you will feel no rain, for each of you will be the shelter for the other.*
> *Now you will feel no cold, for each of you will be the warmth to the other.*
> *Now you are two persons, but there is only one life before you.*
> *Go now to your dwelling to enter into the days of your life together.*
> *And may your days be good and long upon the earth.*
>
> *Dear ones, remember to treat both yourself and each other with respect, and remind yourselves often of what brought you together. Give the highest priority to the tenderness, gentleness, and kindness that your connection deserves. When frustration, difficulty, or fear assail your relationship—as they have threatened all relationships at one time or another—remember to focus on what is right between you, not only on the part that seems wrong.*
>
> *In this way, you can ride out the times when clouds hide the face of the sun in your lives—remembering that even if you lose sight of it for a moment, the sun is still there.*
>
> *And if each of you takes responsibility for the quality of your lives together, your life together will be marked by abundance and delight.*

May peace and joy be with you, now and through all your days.

Shonnie Lavender & Bruce Mulkey

Appendix

Marriage vow examples

The marriage vows below are those created by us and by other couples. With one exception in which the partner is deceased, each of these couples continues to uphold and abide by the commitments they made on their wedding day.

Bruce Mulkey & Shonnie Lavender, May 30, 1999

<u>Bruce to Shonnie</u>

I will join you in full partnership to cocreate the life we both envision.

I will join you in living consciously, purposefully, passionately, congruently.

I will join you in creating true community and a more compassionate world in which to live.

I will laugh and dance and sing and have fun with you.

I will tell you the truth even when I think you might not want to hear it, and I will hear you when you tell me your truth.

I will afford you your humanity and not expect you to always be at your best.

When you forget who you really are, I'll remind you of your power, spirit, integrity, intelligence, creativity, athleticism, and beauty.

I will remember that any anger, resentment, frustration I show toward you is more about me than about you and will refuse to hold ill will toward you.

I will be true to you and honor the commitments that we make to one another for all our days. I will open my heart to you and love you with all my being.

<u>Shonnie to Bruce</u>

I will be authentically me. Bringing all my gifts and challenges and willingly using all the tools I have to fully live out my life's purpose.

I will be your mirror. Reflecting the truth and reminding you of who you are, listening attentively with an open heart and mind as I seek to better understand and support you in fully living your life's purpose.

I will be your helpmate. Willingly sharing our responsibilities and honors, owning my part in creating our life, readily and fully forgiving, and working together to put us back on course when we stray from our path.

I will be your partner. Treating you with respect and equality, being creative and flexible in living interdependently in a way that reflects who we are individually and as a couple.

I will be your lover. Passionate and playful, tender and loyal, sharing myself fully and nurturing our love so that we grow ever more intimate.

I will be your friend. Honest and trustworthy, compassionate and committed, sharing all that life brings us.

I will be your companion. Honoring these sacred vows as we walk together, hand in hand, heart to heart, soul to soul, for all our days, giving all that we have and being all that we are, to create a world full of peace, love, and understanding.

> *Love at first sight is easy to understand; it's when two people have been looking at each other for a lifetime that it becomes a miracle.*
>
> ~Amy Bloom

Elizabeth Trezise-Barbour & Eric Barbour, October 23, 2004

I, Eric/Elizabeth, intend to be faithful, loyal, and trustworthy both as a husband/wife to you and as a parent to our children.

I intend that our marriage be guided gently and steadily by the hand of God.

I intend that we will explore and discover life together with curiosity, wonder, and openness.

I intend that we will make a home together that is grounded and playful as we enjoy the presence of Andy, Percy, Jasper, and Graham!

I intend to honor your needs and to clearly communicate my needs to the best of my ability.

I intend to always seek the goodness and grace within you even when you drive me crazy!

I intend to celebrate you when you're strong and cradle you when you're weak.

I intend to celebrate the uniqueness of you and the union of us.

I intend to nurture the balance of masculine and feminine that makes you whole and complete.

I intend that we will seek the support, guidance, and wisdom of our families and friends through good and challenging times.

May love be the way we live in gratitude as we continue to thank God for all of our blessings.

I will honor these sacred vows as we walk side by side and hand in hand, giving all that we have and being all that we are.

I, Eric/Elizabeth, will open my heart to you, Elizabeth/Eric, and love you with all of my being.

> *In marriage, every day you love, and every day you forgive. It is an ongoing sacrament, love and forgiveness.*
>
> ~Bill Moyers

John & Julie M., April 26, 2003

Julie to John

You fell from the sky into my life,
and I haven't been the same since.

Bright eyes, warm smile,
tender heart, incredible soul,
you've captured my heart.

I promise to love you,
take care of you,
laugh with you and cry with you,
listen to you,
be compassionate to you,
and have fun ... just have fun
living with you,
long after my body goes back to the earth
and my spirit to the sky.

John to Julie

I will lift you up and support you through times of laughter and tears.

At our brightest moments and darkest hours I will be there without judgment.

Compassionate and equanimous, I will be.

I will encourage you in your endeavors and nourish your spirit as we walk through this life together.

As we face the impermanence of our beings and bodies, our love will remain as a force for eternity.

I will always allow you to be you.

I will always love you.

> *A good marriage is one which allows for change and growth in the individuals and in the way they express their love.*
>
> ~Pearl S. Buck

Tracy Hildebrand & Stewart Stokes, September 22, 2001

I, Tracy/Stewart, take you, Stewart/Tracy, to be my husband/wife, and these vows I make to you:

I will share my love with you.

I will nourish, respect, and cherish you with integrity and faithfulness.

I will honor your spiritual growth.

I will protect your solitude.

I will encourage your creative fulfillment.

I will live consciously with gratitude for our blessings.

I will celebrate our life together with laughter and affection.

I will be your friend.

This commitment is made in love, kept in faith, and lived in hope.

> *A kiss is a lovely trick designed by nature to stop speech when words become superfluous.*
>
> ~Ingrid Bergman

Laurey Masterton & Christine Keff, September 25, 2004

Laurey to Christine

Dear Chris,

In my life with you I promise to:

tell you the truth – even when it is very difficult

be careful with you

have a lot of fun

be vulnerable with you

take care of you

laugh a lot

make you feel special

share wine with you

have adventures with you

make love with you – often

kiss you when you are cooking

tell you how much I love you

surprise you

and

be independent

be strong and weak too

take care of myself and let you take care of me

make you soup and eat your soup

set a beautiful table

cook with you

explore new foods with you

explore new worlds with you

build a life with you

have a great time.

Christine to Laurey

Laurey Clark Masterton, daughter of Elsie and John, sister of Lucinda and Heather, aunt to Rachel, friend to many and lover to me, these are the promises I make to you:

I promise to be constant, to remind you of what is at those times when all you can see is what's not.

I promise to slow down, to live in a way that lets me revel in the wonder of you, to leave a space in me that you can enter.

I promise never to stop flirting with you, to remain a little mysterious, to save back some secrets about which you can wonder.

I promise to watch for blue herons, to see the magic around me and bring it home to you.

I promise to let you go, to let you be you without me, and to listen to all the stories when you come back.

I promise to come to my senses, all five of them.

I promise to dance all around the living room, with you and without you, to be joyful.

I promise to trust this happiness and let it flow through me and around me, without question.

I will sing you to sleep, read you a story, make you hot chocolate, and draw you a bath, wash your back. I will find every way to soothe you, to feed you, to let you know what my love feels like. Always. Always, always, always.

> *Love is everything it's cracked up to be. . . . It really is worth fighting for, being brave for, risking everything for. And the trouble is, if you don't risk anything, you risk even more.*
>
> Erica Jong

Elizabeth Pavka & Carroll Thompson, December 28, 1991

In love, we two have become one that we may each nourish the independent expansiveness of the other;

We together seek that higher spirituality which is for all humans;

We acknowledge joy and laughter as the wings of life;

We caress the Earth as our beloved home in space;

We recognize the stars as relatives to the light in us;

We cherish our individuality and our separateness as the binding agents which drew us together as one, yet hold us apart as two;

We affirm all humans are one people, all life one life, all Spirit one Spirit;

We face the frontier of our personal spiritual development with joy;

We now unite our hearts, souls, bodies, energies, minds, senses, and emotions, that we each may more fruitfully serve the higher purposes we have accepted for ourselves;

God is Love. Love is Light. Light is God in us.

We came as two. We go as one. We are in Universal Union.

> *For I tell you this: at the critical juncture in all human relations, there is only one question: What would love do now?*
>
> ~Neale Donald Walsch

Lance & Tricia Secretan, May 29, 1993

I want you to know that I love you,

And I will for the rest of my days.

I will trust and respect you,

Tell the truth and embrace you.

Every day. All the time. And always.

For the rest of our lives together

Every day in your favor I'll bend;

I'll make rain seem like dew -

I'll make you smile when you're blue.

That's forever and ever. Amen.

A successful marriage requires falling in love many times, always with the same person.

~Mignon McLaughlin

David & Deanna LaMotte, June 5, 2004 (private) and July 10, 2004 (public)

David to Deanna

I love you.

And when I tell you I love you, this is what I mean:

You are the one for whom I have waited. You have brought me more peace and steadiness than I have ever known, and the days since I met you have been the best days of my life. Your ready smile, your deep convictions, your passion and compassion, your beauty, your laughter, your sense of adventure, your intelligence, your wisdom, your faith, your courage, your kindness and the lessons of your experience enrich me in every moment I spend with you.

I offer you my history, with its pride and its regret;

My future, walking with you wherever we go;

This present moment, which explodes with more joy than a moment should be able to hold.

All of my joy and fear, my brokenness and my courage, my success and failure, my humor and despair, my loneliness and my connectedness.

I promise to laugh with you and to laugh at myself.

I promise to take you seriously when seriousness is called for.

I promise to hold you while you cry, and to cry while you hold me.

I promise to care for you as best I can, and to encourage you to stretch and grow and care for yourself.

I promise to love and nourish myself, as a child of God and as the one whom you have chosen.

I promise to support you in sharing your gifts with others, to encourage your generosity and your chosen responses to your many callings.

I promise to listen to you, respect and consider your thoughts and beliefs, and to heed your challenges to my own.

I promise to rest with you, and to seek balance between work and play.

I promise to seek God with you, bravely and constantly, holding you closer than any other human to the heart of my heart, with only God in the very center.

I promise you nothing less than the rest of my life. You are my closest friend, and I give you myself. This is what I mean when I tell you that I love you.

From this moment on you are my wife, and, with Divine assistance, I promise to be your loving and faithful husband for the rest of our lives.

Deanna to David

I love you. And when I say I love you, what I mean is...

Everything within me, from the most analytical thoughts (complete with pro/con lists) to the goosebumps and butterflies, and especially the still small Voice, tells me that it is right to commit my life to building a life with you...

...because I believe we are stronger together than we are apart and that we can grow more in our intellect, our compassion, and in our faith together than we could alone.

I promise to stand firm beside you as your partner in pursuing knowledge, adventure, spirituality, peace, and responsibility.

I promise to love and honor who you are rather than who I imagine you to be, and I promise to present myself honestly and openly to you.

I promise to support you when your strength is challenged and to ask for your help in my weakness.

I promise to hold you as completely in my heart in the difficult times as in the joyous ones.

I promise to be open to growth and change and the unexpected as we, as individuals, grow and change.

And, finally, I promise to be open to laughter and wonder and mystery and, most importantly, to God's will in our life together.

You make my joys greater and my sorrows more bearable, and you make my spirit feel known. From this day forward, you are my husband and companion, and I promise, with Divine assistance, to be a loving and faithful wife for the rest of our lives.

> *May the god of your*
> *choice bless you.*
> ~Kinky Friedman

Resources

Books

The Eight Essential Traits of Couples Who Thrive, Susan Page. "The question should not be 'What is a perfect marriage?' but 'What is *your* perfect marriage?' A marriage does not have to conform to any of the common stereotypes of marriage in order to be perfect for the two people who are in it."

***A Return to Love: Reflections on the Principles of* A Course in Miracles**, Marianne Williamson. "Love is what we were born with. Fear is what we learned here. The spiritual journey is the relinquishment, or unlearning, of fear and the acceptance of love back into our hearts."

The Art of Intimacy, Thomas Patrick Malone & Patrick Thomas Malone. ". . . The healthy person, the mature person, is the one who can do just this: remain himself or herself while in relationship to another."

The Five Love Languages: How to Express Heartfelt Commitment to Your Mate, Gary Chapman. "The object of love is not getting something you want but doing something for the well-being of the one you love. It is a fact, however, that when we receive affirming words we are far more likely to be motivated to reciprocate."

Gay and Lesbian Weddings: Planning the Perfect Same-Sex Ceremony, David Toussaint. "Covers *everything* you need to know to plan the wedding of your dreams. Unlike other wedding planners, this one tackles the issues your heterosexual friends never had to consider."

Getting the Love You Want: A Guide for Couples, Harville Hendrix. "Imago (the relationship therapy described in the book) focuses on building trust in relationships by teaching some communication skills which very quickly create a feeling of safety. Many couples immediately experience an opportunity to connect more deeply with their partners, helping them to appreciate them more, and revive the passion and hope in their relationship."

Listening: The Forgotten Skill, Madelyn Burley-Allen. "In this new edition of her classic guide to the art of effective listening, Madelyn Burley-Allen shows you how to acquire active, productive listening skills and put them to work for you—professionally, socially, and personally."

Loving Vows: Inspiring Promises for Building and Renewing Your Marriage, Barbara Eklof. "Cherishing you forever was a promise I happily made at our glorious wedding. Today, I'll vow to master the art of keeping this promise."

The Mastery of Love: A Practical Guide to the Art of Relationship, don Miguel Ruiz. "There are millions of ways to express your happiness, but there is only one way to really be happy, and that is to love. . . . You cannot be happy if you don't love yourself. That is a fact. . . If you do not love yourself, you cannot love anyone else either."

Organic Weddings: Balancing Ecology, Style and Tradition, Michelle Kozin. "*Organic Weddings* fills this gap by providing alternatives to the excessive and synthetic wedding industry machine while still enabling couples to incorporate time-honored traditions, as well as meaningful details that celebrate the bride and groom's own style and values. The book presents new ideas and product information, interviews with eco-leaders, real wedding stories, and tips from eco-brides that can be readily shared with relatives and other wedding decision-makers."

The Seven Principles for Making Marriage Work: A Practical Guide from the Country's Foremost Relationship Expert, John M. Gottman & Nan Silver. "Happily married couples aren't smarter, richer, or more psychologically astute than others. But in their day-to-day lives, they have hit upon a dynamic that keeps their negative thoughts and feelings about each other (which all couples have) from overwhelming their positive ones."

Weddings from the Heart: Contemporary and Traditional Ceremonies for an Unforgettable Wedding, Daphne Rose Kingma. "Marriage is the joining of two lives, the mystical, physical, and emotional union of two human beings who have separate families and histories, separate tragedies and destinies."

Online resources

The Enneagram Institute, www.enneagraminstitute.com. Take the online Enneagram test to determine your personality profile; then use it for personal growth and in your relationship.

Human Rights Campaign, www.hrc.org. An organization working for lesbian, gay, bisexual, and transgender rights. Featuring a special section on the legal aspects of marriage for same sex couples.

Organic Weddings, www.organicweddings.com. Organic Weddings is the most comprehensive wedding planning resource for couples striving to live healthy, natural lifestyles with regard for our environment.

Workshops

Back to Bliss Workshop, www.backtoblissworkshop.com. A workshop presented by Elizabeth Loyd Kinnett and Ken Kinnett that strengthens good relationships and renews those in crisis. In their workshops, created from the experience of their own forty-nine-year relationship, the Kinnetts share the skills that enable them to continue to love each other, love themselves, and nurture their relationship.

Imago Relationship Therapy, www.imagorelationships.org. "Imago Relationship Therapy will help you become aware of the hidden agenda of romantic love, and to see that the conflict in your relationship is a wonderful opportunity for growth. The Imago dialogue provides a safe and supportive set of tools to explore these deep issues with your partner. The emotional bond initially created by romantic love is able to evolve into the powerful, lifelong bond that is real love."

More To Life, www.moretolife.org. "More To Life courses teach practical tools and skills that help you connect with your best self whenever you choose and grasp more of the creative possibilities in every life situation. Use them to create partnerships that are more connecting, work that is more fulfilling, and a life in which you become more of who you are, each day of your life."

New Warrior Training Adventure, www.mkp.org. "The ManKind Project's New Warrior Training Adventure is an intense, transformative men's initiation that invites men to forge a deep conscious connection between head and heart. The NWTA offers men a powerful, challenging opportunity to look at all aspects of their lives in a richly supportive environment." **Woman Within**, www.womanwithin.org, is an affiliated program for women.

State of Grace Document, www.stateofgracedocument.com. Maureen McCarthy and Zelle Nelson have created a radical new alternative to business and personal contracts built on trust and respect. "The beauty of the State of Grace Document is that it provides a way to create a solid foundation at the beginning of a

> *You can give without loving, but you can never love without giving. The great acts of love are done by those who are habitually performing small acts of kindness. We pardon to the extent that we love. Love is knowing that even when you are alone, you will never be lonely again. The greatest happiness of life is the conviction that we are loved— loved for ourselves, or rather, loved in spite of ourselves.*
>
> *~Victor Hugo*

relationship that then sustains us through the middle and into the transition phases with grace and dignity. It truly changes the destiny of the relationship."

About the Authors

Bruce Mulkey and Shonnie Lavender met while training for a marathon in Austin, Texas, in 1995. After participating in a running group together for almost a year, the two decided that they could transcend their three-decade age difference, but not the triple-digit Texas temperatures. Thus they moved with their blended family of cats to the Southern Appalachian Mountains in 1997 to a home near downtown Asheville, North Carolina.

Shonnie and Bruce coauthored *I Do! I Do! The Marriage Vow Workbook* based on their experience of consciously crafting their own marriage vows for their May 30, 1999, wedding, commitments they continue to uphold.

Bruce is a writer who tells powerful, inspirational, evocative stories intended to touch our hearts, minds and spirits, awaken us from complacency, and inspire us to become radically responsible for our lives and our world. He graduated from the University of the South at Sewanee, Tennessee, and has pursued a variety of professions, including high school teacher, log home builder, energy conservation advocate, and nonprofit communications director, before ultimately choosing to follow his true calling—writing.

Bruce's essays and commentaries have appeared in the *Asheville Citizen-Times*, where he served as an editorial columnist from 2000 through 2004, as well as numerous other print and online publications. He currently blogs at www.brucemulkey.com.

Shonnie is a coach and speaker. Her life and work are oriented around her cause: To inspire and empower people to live in a conscious, loving, and connected way. Through empathic listening, evocative inquiry, and compelling calls to action, Shonnie helps her clients embody their authentic power, embrace their accountability, and become the change they want to see in the world.

A graduate of The University of Texas at Austin and Coach U, Shonnie is a member of the International Coach Federation and serves on the faculty of the Secretan Center, a global consulting practice specializing in cultural and leadership transformation. Her clients come from a variety of professional backgrounds, including not-for-profit, communications, law, health care, academia, graphic design, architecture, consulting, and coaching. She also presents workshops, trainings, keynote speeches, group coaching, and telephone-based classes. Shonnie is the author of numerous articles and a book titled *Live the Life You've Imagined: 100 Practical Strategies for Creating Your Ideal Life*.

Shonnie and Bruce continue to run together on nearby mountain trails. Since moving to Asheville, they've twice participated in the grueling eighteen-mile Shut-In Trail Race. And just about every Saturday you'll find them out on a trail somewhere in western North Carolina, Shonnie faster on the uphill grades, Bruce faster on the down-hill, arriving at their destination together . . . in speed and in spirit.

Shonnie and Bruce's wedding from the *Christian Science Monitor*

Below is an excerpt from a story about unique weddings by Jennifer Wolcott that appeared in the *Christian Science Monitor* newspaper on May 3, 2000.

Take Bruce Mulkey and Shonnie Lavender, for instance. The couple, who met while training for a marathon in Austin, Texas, set out to host what they call a "high-tech, high-touch" wedding. It included not only a weekend of hiking, meditation, and music in the Appalachian Mountains, but also an opportunity for their 300 guests to become acquainted before meeting in person. An "eGroup" of the 100-plus guests with e-mail provided an opportunity for these guests to "get to know each other, share stories of how they know us, and form a virtual community before arriving," says Mr. Mulkey.

And their wedding Web site provided a forum for guests to RSVP, get directions, or read about the couple—their significant age difference, common love of nature, and commitment to service.

Technology also helped with organizing their wedding "team," a group of 30 friends and relatives who played an important role during the weekend—from picking up guests at the airport to leading hikes or hosting the men's and women's gatherings.

At the ceremony, two ministers, also friends, first welcomed the guests and then thanked them for "creating this ritual in cyberspace before they'd all met," recalls Mulkey. They read American Indian prayers and poems before and after the vows, shared the couple's thoughts on forgiveness, and afterward, invited the crowd to follow the newlyweds down a hill to water a tree planted that morning in celebration of this union.

"We wanted our friends and family to know us and one another at a deeper level," says Mulkey. "And for them to leave feeling transformed by their participation in the events. The thought of a traditional wedding didn't even occur to us."

An Invitation

Do you want to attend a marriage vow workshop or participate in a teleclass? Do you need help with the precise language of your vows? Would you like to share your completed vows with us and others? Read on to find out how you can do so.

Take a class
We offer teleclasses and workshops on creating marriage vows as well as on other vital relationship issues. Visit www.marriagevowworkbook for a schedule of upcoming events.

Polishing your vows
Need help putting the finishing touches on your marriage vows? Contact us at the e-mail address below to let us know how we might be of service.

Share your feedback and your vows
We'd like to know how *I Do! I Do! The Marriage Vow Workbook* has served you in creating your marriage vows. Your feedback and suggestions, including other resources you recommend, are extremely valuable to us. We also invite you to share your marriage vows as inspiration for other couples as they create theirs. Please visit www.marriagevowworkbook.com for details on how you can do so, or contact us at the e-mail address below.

Order additional copies
To order additional copies of *I Do! I Do! The Marriage Vow Workbook*, visit www.marriagevowworkbook.com. Discounts are available for bulk orders. Please contact us at the e-mail address below for bulk order pricing.

Contact us
Bruce Mulkey & Shonnie Lavender
16 Spears Avenue, #19
Asheville, NC 28801
info@marriagevowworkbook.com
www.marriagevowworkbook.com

> *Marriage is our last, best chance to grow up.*
> ~Joseph Barth

Made in the USA
Middletown, DE
03 March 2020